TEMPERATE CLIMATES

Cath Senker

capstone

Edited by Linda Staniford
Designed by Philippa Jenkins
Original illustrations © Capstone Global Library Limited 2017
Illustrated by Oxford Designers and Illustrators, Gordon Hurden p 6, and Maurizio De Angelis p 17
Picture research by Svetlana Zhurkin
Production by Victoria Fitzgerald
Originated by Capstone Global Library Ltd

20 19 18 17 16
10 9 8 7 6 5 4 3 2 1

Library of Congress Cataloging-in-Publication Data
Library of Congress Cataloging-in-Publication Data is available on the Library of Congress website.
ISBN: 978-1-4846-3782-1 (library hardcover)
ISBN: 978-1-4846-3786-9 (paperback)
ISBN: 978-1-4846-3798-2 (eBook PDF)

This book has been officially leveled using the F&P Text Level Gradient™ Levelling System.

Acknowledgments
We would like to thank the following for permission to reproduce photographs: Alamy: studiomode, 44; Capstone: Gordon Hurden, 6, Maurizio De Angelis, 17, Oxford Designers and Illustrators, 40; Courtesy Matt Jolly, RMRS Missoula Fire Sciences Laboratory, U.S. Forest Service, 41; Dreamstime: Joserpizarro, 31, Natalia Rumyantseva, 11, Susan Sheldon, 12; iStockphoto: NunyaCarley, 24; Minden Pictures: Konrad Wothe, 23, Laurent Geslin, 27, Mark Moffett, 14; Newscom: MCT/Patrick Tehan, 33; Shutterstock: Adriano Kirihara, 32, anatolypareev, 26, Antonio S, 8, Bildagentur Zoonar GmbH, 25, C Jones, 7, Dario Lo Presti, 38, Deatonphotos, 42, DJTaylor, 43, FCG, 39, Harthad, 37, Hurly Z, 18, Jaco Botha, 5, Lorraine Logan, 22, Lyudmila Suvorova, 35, Mary Terriberry, 34, Michelangelo Gratton, 29, miropink, 19, mlorenz, 20, Mps197, 13, My Good Images, 30, P.Burghardt, 15, Peter Kunasz, 9, photka, back cover and throughout, Radu Razvan, 45, Raymond Llewellyn, 16, slava296, 36, Steve Byland, 21, Terry Underwood Evans, 10, ueuaphoto, 28, VRstudio, cover

We would like to thank Dr Sandra Mather, Professor Emerita, Department of Geology and Astronomy, West Chester University, West Chester, Pennsylvania, USA, for her invaluable help in the preparation of this book.

Printed and bound in the USA
010052S17CG

TABLE OF CONTENTS

Some words are shown in bold, **like this**. You can find out what they mean by looking in the glossary.

WHERE ARE THE TEMPERATE CLIMATE ZONES?

It's the middle of summer. In the Mediterranean, it's hot and sunny. In Seattle, Washington, it's mild and rainy. Welcome to temperate climates — the most varied climates in the world.

This map shows the temperate climate zones of the world.

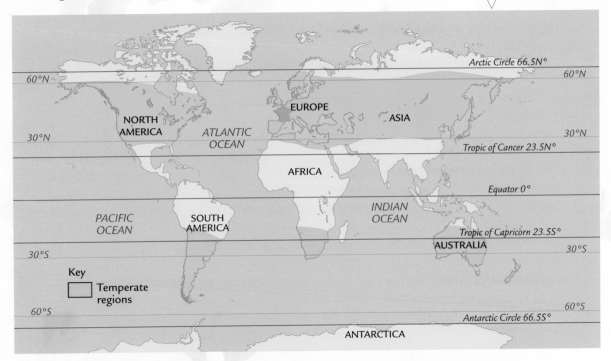

- Arctic Circle 66.5N°
- 60°N
- 60°N
- NORTH AMERICA
- EUROPE
- ASIA
- ATLANTIC OCEAN
- 30°N
- 30°N
- Tropic of Cancer 23.5N°
- AFRICA
- Equator 0°
- PACIFIC OCEAN
- SOUTH AMERICA
- INDIAN OCEAN
- Tropic of Capricorn 23.5S°
- AUSTRALIA
- 30°S
- 30°S
- Key — Temperate regions
- 60°S
- 60°S
- Antarctic Circle 66.5S°
- ANTARCTICA

MARITIME AND CONTINENTAL, COOL AND WARM

The temperate climates are found between the **tropics** and the polar regions. There are two main types of temperate climates: maritime and continental. The maritime climate is influenced by ocean winds and currents. The places with a maritime climate are usually on the western edges of continents and are between 30° and 60° north and south of the Equator. Examples of areas with a maritime climate include western Europe and western North America. Inland areas between the tropics and the polar regions have a continental climate, as do areas between 30° and 60° north of the Equator, in central and eastern North America and Asia.

Temperate continental climates can be divided into warm and cool continental climates. Maritime climates can also be divided into warm and cool maritime climates. A warm maritime, or Mediterranean, climate is found in parts of Spain, Italy, Greece, and Turkey. The southeastern tip of Australia, coastal Norway, and parts of Iceland have a cool maritime, or Marine West Coast, climate.

In the United States, there is a cool continental climate east of the Rockies and north into Canada, from around 40° north. South of around 40° north, there's a warm continental climate. A large strip across central China has a cool continental climate. Eastern China has a warm continental climate.

The comfortable temperatures in the temperate climates have allowed a wide variety of plants and animals to develop. Resources from the land, forests, and seas are plentiful. They're such popular places to live and visit that these regions are under great pressure from people, industry, and agriculture.

Cape Town, South Africa, is an example of an area with a warm maritime climate. These occur along west coasts of continents, generally south of 40° in the northern hemisphere and north of 40° in the southern hemisphere.

WHAT ARE TEMPERATE CLIMATES LIKE?

Temperate climates are cooler than tropical climates. In the temperate zones, the Sun's rays are spread out and strike over a wide area.

Cool maritime zones have four seasons. Yet even in summer, there might be rain, fog, and low temperatures. Summers do tend to be drier than other times of year though. Warm maritime regions are a bit different. Here, there are two seasons: hot, dry summers and cool, rainy winters. Inland, the ocean does not moderate the temperature as it does at the coast (see page 7). In areas with a continental climate, the temperatures are more extreme, with hot summers and cold winters. Inland areas may also experience dramatic weather events, such as severe thunderstorms or **tornadoes.**

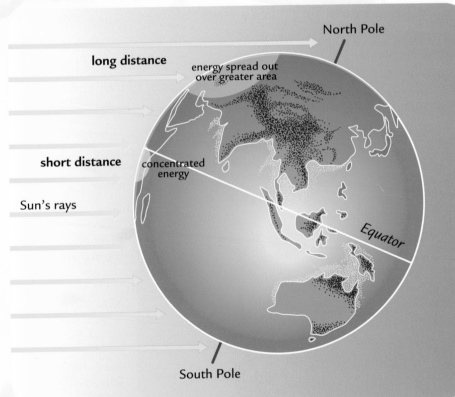

long distance

energy spread out over greater area

North Pole

short distance

concentrated energy

Sun's rays

Equator

South Pole

This diagram shows how the Sun's rays are more spread out in the temperate zones than in the tropics.

DID YOU KNOW?

The tilt of Earth's axis creates the seasons. When the southern hemisphere tilts toward the Sun, the region has summer. The northern hemisphere tilts away from the Sun, and it's winter. Earth turns on its axis and six months later, it's the opposite. The northern hemisphere tilts toward the Sun, and people in that half of the world enjoy summer.

COOL MARITIME CLIMATE: WET AND WINDY

In regions with a cool maritime climate, there is more rain near the coast than inland. That's because these zones are on the west of temperate continents, and winds in temperate zones generally come from the west, bringing rain. On the plus side, the temperatures are milder, so it's not so chilly in winter. The ocean heats up and cools down more slowly than the land. This makes the temperatures on the land at the coast less extreme than the temperatures inland. The water remains cold in summer, keeping the coasts cool, and stays warm into winter, making the land warmer.

Cornwall is on the southwest coast of the United Kingdom. The west coast has more rain than the east coast.

WARM MARITIME CLIMATE

There are five warm maritime, or Mediterranean, regions: the Mediterranean countries; much of California and northern Baja California; the central coast of Chile; southwest and parts of south Australia; and the Cape region of South Africa. These regions have a lot in common. Summers are hot and dry, making perfect beach weather. Most of the rainfall arrives with the short winters. In the coldest month, temperatures are above 27 degrees Fahrenheit (−3 degrees Celsius) and can reach 64°F (18°C). So there's no need for warm winter boots.

Camogli is in northwest Italy, a Mediterranean country. The weather is mild and it rains more in the winter than in the summer. There are also storms in the winter.

Unlike the cool continental zones, where it rains all year round, the Mediterranean regions have wet winters and dry summers. That's because the Mediterranean regions are closer to a **high-pressure cell** that hovers over an ocean. The cells move toward the polar regions in summer, pushing storms away from the land. The **jet streams** push the cells back toward the Equator in winter, bringing storms to the Mediterranean zones.

Mountains: Climate barriers

Mountains act as climate barriers. In North America, the Rocky Mountains run north to south and act as a barrier to the mild maritime winds from the west. To the east, the climate is continental. Yet in Europe the maritime climate stretches farther inland because the large mountain range there, the Alps, runs from west to east. The Alps don't create a climate barrier for winds coming from the Atlantic Ocean into northern Europe.

The Rocky Mountains in Colorado block warm, moist air from reaching the places next to them, such as Denver, so these places have a dry climate.

COOL CONTINENTAL CLIMATE

Closer to the poles, as the **latitude** increases, the climate becomes cooler. The higher latitudes with a cool continental climate include the northern United States; Canada; parts of northern Europe including Russia, Norway, and Finland; and the east coast of Asia — northern Japan and China.

Eyewitness account: Damage from a tornado

One night in Providence, Kentucky, David Bolser was woken up by lightning, high winds, and heavy rain. Suddenly, the power failed and the tornado siren blared. His children were on the other side of town with his wife's parents. Just then, they called, reporting that a tornado had whirled through, but they were fine. Bolser rushed out to help clear the highway, which was covered in fallen trees and debris. Some homes were damaged and a few were completely flattened by the tornado.

A tornado can cause devastation. This is the scene in Tuscaloosa, Alabama, after a tornado hit in April 2011.

In cool continental zones, it never gets particularly warm. Even in the warmest month, the average temperature is below 50°F (10°C), and in the coldest month it plummets to below 27°F (−3°C). Some northern areas such as Russia and Finland have long, cold winters. In St. Petersburg, Russia, the average temperature in January is a chilly 18°F (−8°C).

Ice skating is a popular winter pastime in snowy St. Petersburg, Russia.

WHICH PLANTS LIVE IN THE TEMPERATE REGIONS?

The temperate regions are home to an amazingly varied range of plants. The northern regions of North America, Europe, and Asia have a cool continental climate. In these regions, **coniferous** forests of spruce, hemlock, pine, fir, and larch rise into the sky. Conifers are mostly evergreen — they lose some of their needles each year, but they don't lose all of them in the fall. Conifers here tend to be smaller and grow more slowly than trees in warmer areas.

Few plants grow below the trees because it's so dark. Shade-loving species such as **mosses,** fungi, and some ferns can thrive though. In the gaps in the trees, look for wild flowers, juniper, and other berry bushes.

Firs make good Christmas trees because they keep their needles in the middle of winter.

COOL CONIFERS

Conifers are well adapted to the chilly continental climate. Their **sap** contains a substance that prevents it from freezing in winter. Conifers are usually cone shaped so that winter snow easily slides off them. It's hard for snow to settle on the narrow, pointed needles anyway. The needles tend to be dark to absorb the maximum amount of sunlight. Conifers need to retain as much water as possible too. The roots can't absorb water when the ground is frozen. The needles have a waxy surface so they don't lose much water through **evaporation** into the air.

DID YOU KNOW?

Wildfires happen naturally in many continental and maritime temperate forests. Some trees have thick bark to resist fire. Some pine trees in North America have seeds that remain tightly in their cones until fire or hot, dry winds make the cone scales open, releasing the seeds into a **fertile** ash bed. Amazingly, many plants can regrow after they are burned, from the root or the stem.

A pinecone's scales open after it has been burned in a wildfire.

STUDYING THE SEQUOIA

The giant sequoia grows in the Mediterranean (or warm maritime) coniferous forests of North America. These mammoth trees have huge networks of roots to take in water and **nutrients** and super-thick bark to help them resist forest fires.

THE LEAF TO LANDSCAPE PROJECT

Nathan Stephenson, research **ecologist** for the U.S. Geological Survey, is one of a team of scientists studying the sequoias of Sequoia National Park in California. He explained, "I came out here in autumn 2014 because we'd been having this really severe **drought.**" The team wanted to see which areas of the forest were suffering most, so park managers could decide where to focus their resources.

A researcher swings from one giant sequoia to another in Sequoia National Park.

Amazing fact

Giant sequoias can be more than 300 feet (90 meters) tall – about the length of a football field.

First, Stephenson checked the seedlings, thinking they might have died: "But they all looked pretty healthy." In contrast, much of the **foliage** of the mature trees had died. The team used ground surveys to create maps of the whole area. Then they selected two sites with high levels of needle death and two with low needle death. They measured the water in the needles early in the morning and in the afternoon when they were most water stressed (short of water). This involved climbing 50 trees twice a day for two weeks. They linked their water measurements with airborne data that measured the height and structure of the topmost branches and how much water was in the leaves.

They discovered that the areas of the forest at lower elevations (height above sea level) were the most drought stressed. The sequoias lost foliage to save water and resist the drought. But will they survive major **climate changes** to come?

Some long-living sequoias in Sequoia National Park have been given names. The General Sherman Tree (named after a high-ranking soldier in the Civil War) is thought to be between 2,300 and 2,700 years old.

DECIDUOUS FORESTS

Many thousands of years ago, the warm continental lands were covered with deep, dark forests, just like the ones in fairy tales. Yet since ancient times, many of these forests have been cleared for farmland. Today these **deciduous** forests still stand in eastern North America, eastern Asia, and western Europe.

Deciduous woodlands in the United Kingdom often have a carpet of bluebells. These bloom in spring, before the leaves of the trees are fully grown and there is still plenty of light.

DID YOU KNOW?

The broad leaves of deciduous trees are far tastier to plant-eating animals than the narrow needles of conifers. The leaves are soft and easy to digest.

Deciduous trees have broad leaves to catch the Sun's rays. Spring and summer are the time of growth — a much longer growing season than the conifers in the cold continental regions have. In fall, deciduous trees lose their leaves, so they are bare in winter. The deciduous forest has five layers.

1 Trees
In the tallest layer, 60–100 feet (18–30 m) high, there are trees such as oak, maple, beech, elm, and chestnut.

2 Small trees and saplings
Smaller tree species, such as dogwood and redbud, live here, along with young trees of the larger species.

3 Shrubs
Rhododendron, azalea, and mountain laurel bring some color to the forest. They grow mainly in clearings and at the forest edge, where there is more light.

4 Herbs
Here there are wildflowers, herbs, and berries. In spring, pretty bluebells and wood-sorrel flowers can be seen before the trees grow leaves and shade the forest floor. Then the flowers die back, storing food in their bulbs so they are ready to pop up again the following spring.

5 Ground
On the ground are **lichens** and mosses, which need little sunlight. Fungi such as mushrooms live on dead material. Fungi can be poisonous. They should only be picked by experts who know which ones are safe to eat.

MEDITERRANEAN PLANTS

The strong rays of the Sun in the Mediterranean create excellent growing conditions for plants. The plants have **evolved** special features to survive the long, parched summer.

All the Mediterranean regions have trees and scrubland — there are shrubby evergreen plants, with small, leathery leaves to reduce water loss. The dense shrubs include heath and sweet-smelling lavender and thyme. These plants are often grown in gardens in warm temperate regions.

Proteas are typical plants of the fynbos, the Mediterranean region of South Africa.

Survival strategies

The biggest danger for plants is the evaporation of water through their leaves. They have evolved cunning ways to solve this problem. As summer approaches, sage loses its winter leaves and sprouts small summer leaves, which curl and produce oil to reduce evaporation. Grazing goats find the taste of the oil disgusting, so they leave the sage alone.

Capers have a salty flavor and are used in cooking. They are the unopened flower buds of the caper plant, which grows wild in the Mediterranean climate region. It has strong suction in its roots so it can suck in moisture from the soil. The caper flowers in hours. It produces blossoms at night so they don't shrivel in the Sun. By dawn, the flower is open, attracting bees. By midday, it is dead. But the next night there will be another. The caper produces one bud every night for the entire flowering season.

This is a caper plant in bloom. An unopened bud can be seen to the right. Capers appear in the wild, but gardeners and farmers can also grow them.

WHICH ANIMALS LIVE IN THE TEMPERATE REGIONS?

The forests and woodlands of the temperate regions have a wide variety of wildlife. Deer, squirrels, snakes, foxes, and eagles can be seen in all the temperate zones, but some creatures prefer either cool or warm temperate climates.

CONIFEROUS FOREST LIFE

The cool continental forests are home to many mammals. They range from hooved creatures, such as moose, deer, reindeer, and caribou, to rodents, including mice, voles, and squirrels. Several mammal predators feed on them, including wolves, lynxes, bears, foxes, snakes, and wolverines (a small, fierce type of weasel).

The markings on a bobcat's fur help it blend into the landscape when hunting prey.

Predators often have to travel long distances to find prey. The bobcat mostly feeds at night on small rodents such as lemmings, voles, and birds. It has fur for warmth on those long night journeys. The athletic marten (a weasel-like mammal) leaps from branch to branch to catch squirrels and birds. Up in the sky, owls, hawks, and northern shrikes search for prey.

Plant-eating birds have specially adapted beaks for forest feeding. The tough, waxy needles of conifers are tough and tricky to eat. But the seeds inside the cones make a nourishing meal. The crossbill has a crossed beak like a pair of pliers to pick out seeds from pinecones and fir cones. The nutcracker, a larger bird, crushes cones with a strong bite to get to the seeds.

In spring, the warmer temperatures bring out mosquitoes, caterpillars, wasps, bees, and sawflies. Insects and snails crawl on lichens and mosses on trees. In North America, carpenter ants make colonies in living and dead trees and logs.

A crossbill lands on pinecones. The baby birds are not born with crossed bills, but they cross as the bird grows.

During winter in the cool continental zone, it is cold and heavy snow falls. Some birds have migrated (moved) south for the season. How do other animals cope?

Feast and famine

Shrews, voles, squirrels, and some birds hide food to provide meals during the cold months. In winter they burrow under the snow to find their stash. Other animals manage to forage for their dinner. Moose and deer munch mosses, lichens, bark, and the shoots of bushes.

In summer, bears eat lots of berries and salmon to fatten up for winter.

Warm winter coat

Some mammals stay cozy by growing thick winter coats. The bobcat also changes its coat to provide **camouflage.** In summer, it is light brown with dark spots, like the branches, and in winter, it turns to a pale gray to match the winter scenery. The ermine also changes its coat — the farther north it lives, the whiter its winter coat.

Amazing fact

The tufted titmouse hoards food in the fall and winter. It hides just one seed at a time, usually shelling it first.

A hedgehog in Germany hibernates for the winter.

Long winter sleep

Woodchucks, hedgehogs, bats, and some bears avoid the cold weather altogether by hibernating. When an animal hibernates, its body temperature drops and its heart rate and breathing slow, to save energy. It survives on fat built up in the summer. The dormouse wakes up occasionally to eat a snack that it has stored.

In winter, wasp, bee, and sawfly pupae (at the stage between the larva and adult stage) bury themselves in the ground or in tree trunks for warmth. If they're unlucky, a woodpecker will dig them out for dinner.

CONTINENTAL DECIDUOUS FORESTS

The diverse animals of the deciduous forests have adapted to feed and nest in and around the trees.

Forest dwellers

Deer are not easy to spot. They usually move quietly through the trees, and their coats are brown for camouflage so they don't attract predators. The fawns are born in spring, when there is plenty of foliage to eat; they grow strong in summer. Their spotted coats make them hard to see.

Grizzly bears should be avoided. They can be aggressive, especially in spring, when they have young cubs.

These deer are perfectly camouflaged in the woodland. In winter, they survive on fallen leaves, twigs, and woody plants.

Amazing fact

Some unusual animals live in deciduous forests. The opossum is the only marsupial in North America. Marsupials are animals that have pouches for their babies. Most marsupials live in and around Australia. Another strange animal is the woodlouse. Although it looks like an insect, it is actually a crustacean. A crustacean has a body with three sections and a hard outer shell, and most of them live in the sea. The woodlouse is one of very few kinds of crustacean that lives on land.

In the United States, raccoons live in wooded areas near water. They have long, curved claws to cling to the trees. Highly skilled climbers, they can climb down a tree forward as well as backward.

The juicy tree leaves make good meals for insects, while rotting leaves on the forest floor provide food for woodlice. Predators such as ladybugs and beetles arrive to feed on the insects. Of course, birds use the trees too. Woodpeckers tap holes to dig out food or make nests. The woodpecker has long, curved claws to cling on to the trunk and a thick bill to dig for insects, which it captures with its extraordinarily long, strong, sticky tongue.

A woodpecker searches for a meal.

CITY ANIMALS

People have taken over large areas of temperate habitats to build towns and cities. Many animals and birds have moved in too, attracted by all the waste food and the easy places to nest.

CITY LIFE

Parks, ponds, and lakes are perfect for water birds. Swans, geese, and ducks paddle on the water. Rats like any cold, wet environment. With their excellent eyesight, they settle in underground sewers. Many small rodents, reptiles, and insects find shelter in gaps and holes in buildings.

Just like people, animals often have to downsize in the city. Rabbit burrows are much smaller and house fewer rabbits than in the countryside. English foxes have a reduced territory for hunting.

Rats eat all kinds of food and will also eat food waste in garbage cans, bird food, uneaten pet meals, and even dog poop.

DID YOU KNOW?

Some species of animals have learned to cross the road. Coyotes sit and wait for the traffic to stop. They know which direction the cars are coming from and look before they cross the road.

In the city, there's no shortage of food. Foxes feed on small mammals and food waste, while pigeons feast on crumbs dropped in the street and peck garden vegetables. Some animals have changed their feeding habits to fit with city life. In Thailand and New York, sparrows feed at night, when the bright lights attract the insects they love to eat.

A European brown bear and its cubs search for a meal among garbage cans.

BIG AND HEALTHY

Some species do better in cities than in the rural areas. Author Tristan Donovan has shown that red foxes in urban areas are fatter than their countryside cousins because there's so much waste food around. Urban bears are heavier too because they enjoy a generous buffet of leftovers and prey.

HOW DO PEOPLE USE RESOURCES IN TEMPERATE CLIMATES?

USING THE LAND

Both cool and warm maritime and continental climates are suitable for growing a wide variety of crops. In the countryside there are crops all around. Some areas have large-scale farms using lots of machinery to plant, spray, and harvest the crops. In other places there are small-scale farms with many workers.

Cool continental crops

In the cool continental regions there are fields of wheat, oats, barley, rye, and millet. Leafy vegetables such as spinach don't need hot sunshine to grow. Neither do brassicas — cauliflower, broccoli, and cabbage — or root vegetables such as carrots and potatoes. Pears, apples, and soft fruit are grown to eat fresh or to be made into jams and other tasty sweet products.

Plums are just one kind of soft fruit that grows well in cool continental regions.

Mediterranean riches

In the Mediterranean zones, snow-free winters allow longer growing seasons and a wide range of foods to grow. Farmers can grow avocadoes, eggplants, tomatoes, almonds, and citrus fruit. They harvest olives to eat and to make olive oil, which is used in all kinds of Mediterranean dishes. In Spain and Italy, olive oil is used in pasta, paella, and salads. All the Mediterranean regions are major wine producers too. The wine grapes thrive in the hot, dry summers and mild winters.

Going fishing

Most of the fish we eat probably comes from cool temperate seas — Atlantic herring, cod, halibut, mackerel, and salmon. Mussels, lobsters, and crabs are caught too. But overfishing is a major problem. The United Nations Food and Agriculture Organization reported that in 2011, only 71 percent of fish stocks were being fished **sustainably** — almost one-third weren't being replaced by new fish. Our fish supplies are being rapidly reduced.

USING THE FORESTS

Wood is used for many things around the home. Tables, chairs, pencils, and paper all come from forests. Wood is used for buildings too.

Few people live in the forests. Most temperate forests are managed to control the use of resources and care for the environment. They are popular with visitors though, who enjoy walking, camping, and bird watching among the trees. Mountain bikers race along the forest paths.

In European countries, there are strict rules for managing temperate forests in a sustainable way that does not damage the environment.

Constructing from conifers

We get softwoods from coniferous forests. Cedar is used for boat building, while cypress is strong and doesn't rot easily, so it's great for wooden posts in fields. Pine is long-lasting and good for making toys, boxes, floors, and beams.

Cork

The Mediterranean forests provide **timber**, fruit, and fungi. Cork oaks in southern Europe and north Africa produce cork in their bark. It can be harvested without cutting down the trees and used for wine-bottle stoppers. But today, wine producers often use plastic corks. If cork becomes less important to the economy, people could abandon the forests or cut down the beautiful cork oaks.

Cork is harvested in this forest in Andalucía, southern Spain.

GROWING ORGANIC STRAWBERRIES

Fields of juicy red strawberries look delicious as they ripen in the sunshine. Unfortunately, pests love strawberries too, and they often reach the ripe fruit before the farmers. Most strawberry farmers use **pesticides** to kill the insects. Some of the pesticides the farmers spray drift into the air or enter the soil and can be harmful to people's health, particularly growing children.

Strawberry farmers wear protective gear from head to toe to spray pesticides to protect the fruit.

DID YOU KNOW?

If a farmer plants the same crop in the same field each year, diseases that affect that plant build up in the soil. Moving the plant to another site makes it harder for unwanted pests to infect that crop the following year. Moving crops around each year is known as crop rotation.

Jim Cochran of Swanton Berry Farm believes in working toward a sustainable food system in California.

GOING ORGANIC

Around the world, some farmers have turned to **organic** agriculture to avoid artificial (unnatural) chemicals. In the United States, Jim Cochran runs Swanton Berry Farm in Davenport, California, as an organic farm. Although he's known for his strawberries, he grows mostly vegetables. Cochran uses a seven-year crop rotation, moving each crop to a different field each year. This makes it harder for pests and diseases to damage the strawberries.

To increase sales, Cochran allows customers to come to the farm to pick their own strawberries. He sells treats such as strawberry shortcake, strawberry lemonade, and organic berry jam. Cochran also sells his produce at farmers' markets in the region.

However, switching to organic production is a risky business, and farmers are only likely to switch to organic methods if they are sure they will make money. In the United States, organic strawberry production doubled between 2012 and 2014, but still only makes up 9 percent of the market.

WHAT ARE THE THREATS TO THE TEMPERATE REGIONS?

DISAPPEARING FORESTS

Europe was once covered with vast forests. But only a fraction of the ancient European forests remain. They've been cleared for timber, houses, road building, and farms. Some of those that are left are home to threatened or endangered species of plants and animals.

ACID RAIN AND AGRICULTURE

Industry and pollution can harm forests hundreds of miles away. That's because the smoke and fumes from vehicles and power stations rise into the air and the clouds. They make the moisture in the clouds acidic. The wind blows the clouds to other regions and even other countries. When the moisture falls it produces "acid rain." It damages leaves, causes trees to produce fewer and smaller seeds, and makes them less able to resist disease. Acid rain has been disastrous for coniferous forests in Europe and North America. Wildfires and diseases caused by fungi add to the problems.

Acid rain strips the nutrients from the leaves of trees so they decay and die.

Amazing fact

Half of the tropical rain forest has been preserved from development, but only one-eighth of the original Mediterranean habitat has been protected.

Temperate deciduous forests are also affected by the growth of towns and agriculture. Deciduous forests are particularly popular for timber production because the trees produce hardwoods, which are stronger than tropical softwoods.

Big populations

People are by far the biggest menace to the natural environment of the Mediterranean climate zones. They have flocked to these pleasant regions to live. More than 40 percent of Mediterranean land area has been taken over by cities or turned into farmland. This development has come at a heavy cost to the environment.

San Francisco is just one of the huge cities that migrants have built in Mediterranean regions.

PRESSURE ON WATER SUPPLIES

Adding to the 300 million people who live in the Mediterranean basin, another 220 million tourists visit every year. They come to enjoy the wide golden beaches, warm water, and beautiful weather. The tourist industry makes heavy use of resources, with its golf courses and hotel swimming pools. In the long, hot summers, fresh water is a precious resource, and sometimes there are shortages.

These luxury hotel pools are in Crete, Greece. Crete has an average of just one day a month of rain in June, July, and August.

CLIMATE-CHANGE ALERT

In warm and cold continental regions, climate change could cause more droughts, heat waves, and wildfires. In the Mediterranean regions, the climate is likely to become hotter and drier. At the moment, snow builds up in winter and melts to provide water for the forests in the summer. With higher temperatures, there will be less snowfall, reducing the water supply. If summers are hotter, more water will evaporate into the atmosphere too. Plants will be water stressed and find it harder to cope with damage from pests, disease, and forest fires.

DID YOU KNOW?

Sometimes by accident, people bring exotic plants to new areas. With no natural competitors, the plants can spread quickly, soon covering the landscape. Such invasive species are perhaps the greatest threat to the native plants in the Mediterranean regions, and they're a problem in continental deciduous forests too. The Monterey pine was brought to Chile for lumber, and now it's the dominant forest tree in coastal areas. In Portugal, the Hottentot fig (shown below), an exotic shrub from South Africa, has replaced native plants. Invasive animals can cause trouble too. In 2016 farmers in the United Kingdom were concerned about diamondback moths from Europe threatening to destroy their cauliflower and cabbage crops.

SURVIVAL OF THE FITTEST

In the long term, the types of trees in temperate climates will change. Those that can survive in the new conditions will thrive while others die out. Fierce droughts could destroy some Mediterranean forests, turning them into scrub or grassland within decades. In a parched climate, wildfires could be more frequent and severe.

Climate change can affect people too. If droughts are more frequent, farmers will need more water for their crops, and water shortages will become more common.

Over time, a severe drought could kill the trees in this parched Mediterranean landscape.

❓ DID YOU KNOW?

Simply planting trees may not be the answer to climate change. They need to be the right kinds of trees in the right places. Researchers from France found that some European countries had decided to switch from planting deciduous to coniferous trees. The conifers have dark-colored leaves that absorb more sunlight, keeping in the heat. Water does not evaporate as quickly from their leaves, so the air stays warmer and drier. Planting conifers in areas where deciduous trees grew naturally did not help to reduce the impact of climate change.

Drought, wildfires, pests, and disease

Scientists predict that in the cool continental climate of eastern Europe, global warming will be greatest in winter. The milder temperatures could extend the growing season. That might be good for the conifers. But summer would bring more droughts and forest fires, or wildfires. Where trees are already suffering from losing leaves to drought or damage by pests or disease, those wildfires could be more devastating than usual. Severe fires could kill wildlife and cause many native species to die out, giving way to ones that can cope with warmer temperatures.

Wildfires, like this one in a pine forest, can spread at up to 14 miles (23 km) per hour, destroying everything in their path.

INVESTIGATING THE GLOBAL THREAT OF WILDFIRES

A fire needs three things: something to ignite it, fuel, and air. In some areas, climate change leads to higher temperatures, less rainfall, and higher wind speeds, which all make it easier for fires to burn.

Fire sciences ecologist Matt Jolly works at a research station in Missoula, Montana. His team uses historical data and the latest technology to study the alarming increase in wildfires worldwide.

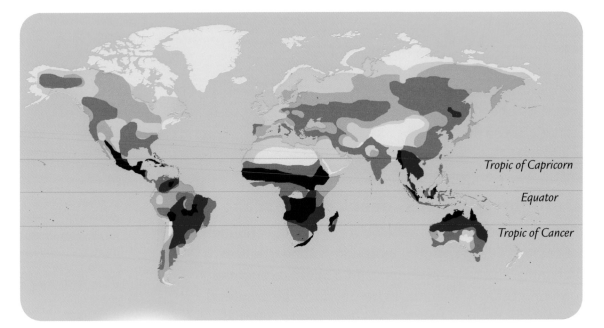

Tropic of Capricorn

Equator

Tropic of Cancer

This map shows areas prone to wildfires. The darker areas show the regions where wildfires are more likely to occur.

Amazing fact

Researchers have discovered that the global area affected by long fire seasons doubled from 1979 to 2013.

Matt Jolly and his team study fire in the lab and outside. This is a controlled burn in Oahu, Hawaii.

FIRE IN THE LAB

Jolly carries out experiments in a combustion (burning) lab to show how wildfires affect the trees. He lights a burner with propane gas. Both the air source and the gas are measured so he knows exactly how much gas and how much air are present. He adds more air to the flame so it is mostly yellow, like a wildfire flame. Its temperature rises to more than 1,832°F (1,000°C).

Then Jolly introduces a sample of spruce needles to the flame. He starts a timer so he will know how long the sample is heated. "The spruce needles are like little rockets," says Jolly. When they are heated, the water inside them expands, building up pressure. The water has to come out somewhere — and it shoots dramatically out of the stem. Researchers then check the moisture content and chemistry of the sample to find out how spruce leaves are changed in a wildfire.

The studies demonstrate the problems caused by the increasing number and severity of wildfires. The problems include damage to the forests from more frequent burning and rising carbon dioxide **emissions** that contribute to climate change.

HOW CAN WE PROTECT THE TEMPERATE ZONES?

Climate change does not only affect places with extreme climates. Temperate zones need to be protected too.

These regions have a high population. Although roads, buildings, and farms are necessary, people should defend nature too and set aside parks and nature reserves.

RESIST INVASION

People should become more aware of species that are a threat to the temperate climate zones. It is best to take steps to try to stop the introduction of invasive plants or animals. Once an invasive species has taken root, it's hard to control it. In the United States, billions of dollars are spent each year on pest control.

DID YOU KNOW?

In temperate deciduous woodlands, coppicing is an ancient way of cutting a tree back to a stump, so that the wood regrows from the stump. Coppicing can be done again and again, and the trees live longer and are more productive. It provides lots of fast-growing, **sustainable** wood without needing to replant trees from seed.

BE WATER WISE

Saving water is vital in areas that are prone to drought. Gray water from showers and washing dishes can be used to water plants and gardens. The watering of public lawns can be limited. Some plants resist drought but are also attractive. Sage and rosemary have a nice scent, and you can cook with them too.

PRACTICE SUSTAINABLE FORESTRY

Trees should be used sustainably. Trees that are cut down must be replaced with suitable trees for the habitat. People should become more aware of the risks of forest fires so they don't start them by accident.

A rain barrel allows gardeners to collect rainwater for their plants. Rainwater is better for the plants and saves water too.

WHAT CAN WE DO?

You can act to protect temperate zones every day. You can buy recycled paper and always use both sides before recycling it. Instead of using paper napkins, plates, and cups, find reusable ones. When your family buys wood products, look for the Forest Stewardship Council (FSC) label, which means the wood comes from a sustainable source.

These tissues are made from a sustainable source. It is even better to buy sustainable tissues in a cardboard box, to avoid plastic packaging.

What if we do nothing?

If we do nothing, in other regions around the world, tropical rain forests will be destroyed and deserts will spread. People will migrate from these damaged areas into temperate climate zones, and the population will continue to grow. Droughts will increase, putting pressure on native plants, animals, and food production. Increasing wildfires will add to the destruction.

Best-case scenario

Things will improve if we adopt methods to protect our environment. We replant forests and reduce water use for farming, industry, and homes. We source our energy from wind, tidal, and solar power, causing less pollution and reducing acid rain. People live sustainably from the land, ensuring there will be resources for future generations.

Try to walk or cycle when you can because car exhaust gives off gases that can cause acid rain.

GLOSSARY

camouflage the way in which an animal's color or shape matches its surroundings and makes it difficult to spot

climate change changes in Earth's weather, including changes in temperature, wind patterns, and rainfall

coniferous to do with a tree that produces hard, dry fruit called cones

deciduous to do with a tree or bush that loses its leaves every year

drought long period with little or no rain, leading to a shortage of water

ecologist someone who studies how plants and living creatures relate to each other and their environment

emissions gases that are sent out into the air

evaporate change from a liquid to a gas

evolve develop over time into forms that are better adapted to survive changes in the environment

fertile land or soil where plants grow well

foliage leaves of a tree or plant

high-pressure cell area of dry, falling air that causes dry weather, except for occasional thunderstorms

jet stream strong wind that blows high in the atmosphere and has an effect on the weather

latitude distance of a place north or south of the Equator, measured in degrees

lichen very small gray or yellow plant that spreads over the surface of rocks, walls, and trees and does not have any flowers

moss small green or yellow plant without flowers

nutrient substance that is vital for a plant or animal to live and grow

organic kind of farming that does not use artificial (unnatural) chemicals on the crops

pesticide chemical used for killing pests, especially insects

sap liquid in a plant or tree that carries food to all its parts

sustainable way of doing things that does not destroy natural resources

timber trees that are grown to be used in building or for making things

tornado a funnel cloud descending from storm clouds, with violent winds whirling around in a circle.

tropics area between the Tropic of Cancer north of the Equator and the Tropic of Capricorn, south of the Equator

READ MORE

BOOKS

Gardner, Robert. *Temperate Forest Experiments: 8 Science Experiments in One Hour or Less.* Berkeley Heights, N.J.: Enslow Elementary, 2015.

Heos, Bridget. *Do You Really Want to Visit a Temperate Forest?* Mankato, Minn.: Amicus Illustrated, 2015.

Johansson, Philip. *The Temperate Forest: Discover This Wooded Biome.* Berkeley Heights, N.J.: Enslow Elementary, 2015.

FACTHOUND

Use Facthound to find Internet sites related to this book.
Just type in 9781484637821 and go!

PLACES TO VISIT

Sequoia and Kings Canyon National Parks, California
https://www.nps.gov/seki/index.htm
See dramatic mountains and canyons and the world's largest trees.

Yellowstone National Park, Wyoming (with parts in Idaho and Montana)
https://www.nps.gov/yell/index.htm
See hundreds of animal species, including wolves, bison, bears, and antelope.

Yosemite National Park, California
https://www.nps.gov/yose/index.htm
Explore waterfalls, meadows, deep valleys, and giant sequoias.

INDEX